Wild Animals Coloring Book for Kids

By: Tomeu D.F.

this book belongs to:

....

....

How to use this book

Welcome to "Wild Animals Coloring Book for Kids"! This book is designed for children to have fun coloring beautiful wild animals from around the world while learning about them. Each page presents a creative and educational challenge.

- On the left pages, you will encounter a black background with the animal information in white color text.

- On the right pages, you will encounter the illustration for coloring.

- Don't forget to use the "tip color" that the left page gives to you and unleash the artist within you!
- Learn and enjoy coloring that 40 beauty wild animals!

From the author:

As a nature enthusiast and animal lover, I have created this book with the hope of inspiring children to explore and learn about the amazing world of wildlife through art and color.

Each illustration has been carefully crafted to capture the beauty and diversity of the animals that share our planet.

I hope you enjoy coloring and learning with this book as much as I enjoyed creating it. Let your imagination soar!

If you want to make any suggestions about the book or if you have any issues, feel free to write to the email address support@tomeudf.com.

Tomeu D.F.

I value your opinion and would appreciate it if you could share it with me and other customers. If you have a moment, I would be grateful if you could leave a review on the book's Amazon page. Thank you very much for your support.

★ ★ ★ ★ ★

Color Test Page

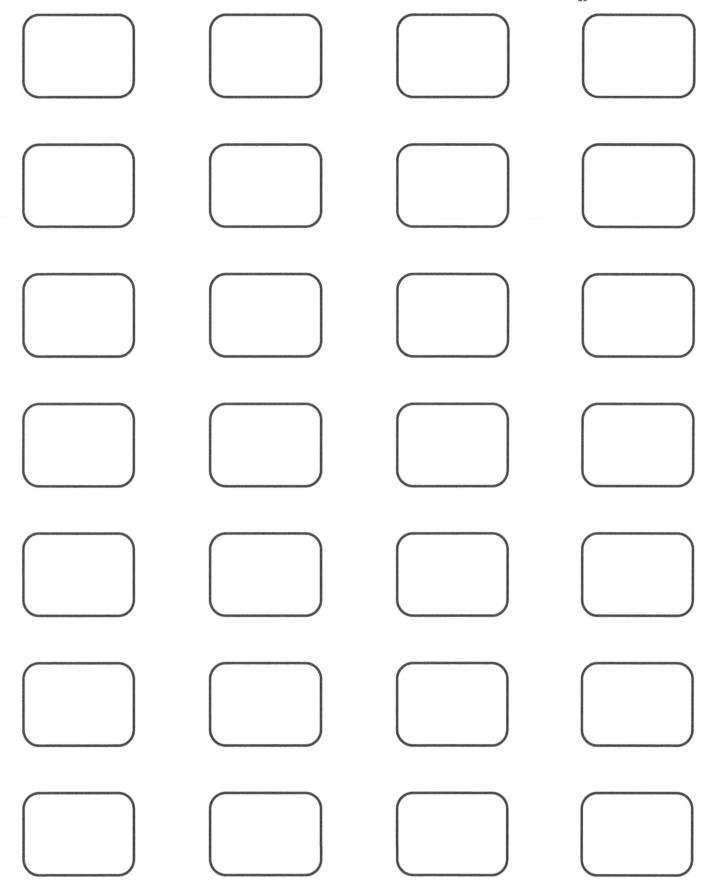

Wild Animals Coloring Book
For Kids

Take your FREE gift!

As a token of appreciation for purchasing this book, follow the QR for a gift you won't want to miss.

Two FREE coloring books:

Or... send an email to
gifts@tomeudf.com
with the word:
'WILDGIFT'

LION

- Class: Mammalia
- Order: Carnivora
- Family: Felidae
- Origin: Africa

Lions are like the brave kings and queens of the savanna, known for their golden manes and mighty roars. These big cats live in family groups called prides and love to play and nap in the warm sun. With sharp claws and powerful jaws, they're top hunters of the animal kingdom.

COLOR TIP

Start with a golden mane that covers the head and neck. then add the body, legs and tail in a lighter shade of yellow or brown.

ELEPHANT

- Class: Mammalia
- Order: Proboscidea
- Family: Elephantidae
- Origin: Africa and Asia

Elephants are the gentle giants of the savanna and forest, with big ears and long trunks, always exploring with their families. Their trunks can do amazing things, from picking up tiny leaves to splashing water for a bath. Elephants love to communicate with rumbles and trumpets.

COLOR TIP

Use a dark gray or black pencil to outline the body, ears and trunk. Then fill in the details with lighter shades of gray or brown, leaving some white spaces for highlights.

GORILLA

- Class: Mammalia
- Order: Primates
- Family: Hominidae
- Origin: Africa

Gorillas are the strong and friendly giants of the jungle, with black fur and big, kind eyes. They live in family groups and love to swing from trees and munch on plants. Gorillas are super smart and can learn sign language to talk to humans.

COLOR TIP

Use a black pencil to outline the body, head and limbs. Then fill in the details with dark gray or brown, leaving some white spaces for highlights.

GIRAFFE

- Class: Mammalia
- Order: Artiodactyla
- Family: Giraffidae
- Origin: Africa

Giraffes are like the tall and elegant wonders of the dry savannahs of Africa, with long necks and unique spots. They're the world's tallest animals, and their long tongues help them reach leaves high in the trees. Giraffes have calm and gentle personalities.

COLOR TIP

Giraffes have patches of orange or brown on a cream background. Paint their spots with various shades to make them stand out.

CROCODILE

- Class: Reptilia
- Order: Crocodylia
- Family: Crocodylidae
- Origin: the Americas, Asia, Africa, and Australia

Crocodiles are the stealthy swimmers of the rivers, with tough scales that protect them from predators and sharp teeth that can crush bones. They like to sunbathe near the water and snap up fish that swim by. Crocs are ancient reptiles and have been around for millions of years.

COLOR TIP

Use an olive green color for its body. Darken its back to show its scales and keep its belly lighter to reflect the sunlight.

GRIZZLY BEAR

- Class: Mammalia
- Order: Carnivora
- Family: Ursidae
- Origin: North America, Europe, and Asia

Grizzly bears are the mighty rulers of the wilderness, with humps and a fearsome presence. They're strong and can be excellent swimmers. Grizzlies are known for their power and independence, as they can defend themselves from other predators.

COLOR TIP

Use a brown color for its fur. Give it a mix of light and dark browns to show its grizzled appearance, which comes from having white or blond tips on its hairs.

IBERIAN LYNX

- Class: Mammalia
- Order: Carnivora
- Family: Felidae
- Origin: Iberian Peninsula

the Iberian Lynx is like a furry friend from a fairy tale. With cute tufted ears and speckled fur, they're the rarest cats in the world. these wild cats are amazing at jumping and love to play hide and seek in the forest.

COLOR TIP

use golden-brown for the fur, dark brown or black for the distinctive spots, and don't forget the white patches on the throat and chest. Make their eyes come alive with shades of green.

RHINO

- Class: Mammalia
- Order: Perissodactyla
- Family: Rhinocerotidae
- Origin: Africa and Asia

Rhinos are like the armored tanks of the grasslands, with a big horn and strong skin. they're big, strong, and love to take mud baths to keep cool. Rhinos are plant-eaters and use their horns to protect themselves and for social interactions, such as fighting for mates or territory.

COLOR TIP

Rhinos are gray with thick skin. Combine light and dark grays to showcase their rugged texture.

WOLF

- Class: Mammalia
- Order: Carnivora
- Family: Canidae
- Origin: North America, Europe, Asia, and Africa

Wolves are the clever hunters of the forests, with gray fur and a howling song. They live in family groups called packs and work together to find food. Wolves are fast runners and have a keen sense of smell.

COLOR TIP

Wolves come in various shades of gray, brown, and sometimes include white tonal variations. To capture the beauty of their fur, it's recommended to use a blend of various grays, browns, and subtle white tones.

BALD EAGLE

- Class: Birds
- Order: Accipitriformes
- Family: Accipitridae
- Origin: North America

Bald eagles are strong and proud birds of America, known for their white heads and powerful wings. They're a symbol of freedom in the United States. These impressive birds build nests that can be as heavy as a car!

COLOR TIP

Bald eagles typically have a white head and tail with a brown body, but some may appear darker or even black. To bring out their distinctive features, use these colors in your artwork.

PENGUIN

- Class: Birds
- Order: Sphenisciformes
- Family: Spheniscidae
- Origin: Antarctica, S. America, Africa, Australia, and New zealand

Penguins are the adorable, tuxedo-wearing birds of the icy seas. they waddle on land but become amazing swimmers when they dive into the water. Penguins are like underwater acrobats and can catch fish with their sleek moves.

COLOR TIP

Penguins are primarily black and white. Make their feathers stand out with sharp black and white contrasts.

MACAW

- Class: Birds
- Order: Psittaciformes
- Family: Psittacidae
- Origin: Central and South America

Macaws are like nature's own artists, showing off feathers as colorful as a rainbow. They love to sing and talk in their own parrot language. These playful birds are expert tree swingers and enjoy munching on delicious, high-up fruits in the treetops.

COLOR TIP

Macaws are like living rainbows. To capture their stunning plumage, use bold and bright colors such as vibrant reds, blues, and yellows.

HIPPOPOTAMUS

- Class: Mammalia
- Order: Artiodactyla
- Family: Hippopotamidae
- Origin: Africa

Hippos are the hefty swimmers of the rivers, with big mouths and a love for mud baths. they're strong swimmers and spend a lot of time in the water. Hippos are known for their big yawns and sharp teeth.

COLOR TIP

Hippos are grayish with pinkish skin. Add pinkish undertones to capture their unique coloring.

POISON DART FROG

- Class: Amphibia (Amphibians)
- Order: Anura
- Family: Dendrobatidae
- Origin: Central and South America

Poison dart frogs may be tiny, but they're big on colors. Some have skin so poisonous that Indigenous people used their toxins for blow darts. But don't worry, they're completely harmless in books or behind glass.

COLOR TIP

Poison dart frogs are brightly colored. their vibrant hues, such as bright red, blue, or yellow, can be a fun challenge to recreate.

MOOSE

- Class: Mammalia
- Order: Artiodactyla
- Family: Cervidae
- Origin: North America, Europe, and Asia

Moose are the tall and goofy walkers of the northern forests, with big antlers and a friendly demeanor. they're herbivores, eating plants and enjoying the outdoors. Moose are known for their unique looks and large size.

COLOR TIP

Moose are typically brown. Layer various shades of brown to make their large bodies come to life.

KOALA

- Class: Mammalia
- Order: Diprotodontia
- Family: Phascolarctidae
- Origin: Australia

Koalas are the furry tree huggers of Australia, with big noses and a love for eucalyptus leaves. They spend most of their time in trees, sleeping and eating. They are marsupials, carrying their babies in a pouch during their early months, and upon emerging, the young koalas cling to their mother's back.

COLOR TIP

Koalas have soft, gray fur with a white chest. To capture their cuddly appearance, blend shades of gray and white.

CLOWNFISH

- Class: Actinopterygii
- Order: Perciformes
- Family: Pomacentridae
- Origin: Pacific and Indian Oceans

Clownfish are like the colorful jokers of the coral reefs, with bright stripes and a protective home. They live in sea anemones and work together to stay safe. Clownfish are great swimmers and live in warm oceans.

COLOR TIP

Clownfish are vibrant orange with white stripes. Use sharp oranges and whites to make them pop.

LEOPARD

- Class: Mammalia
- Order: Carnivora
- Family: Felidae
- Origin: Africa and Asia

Leopards are the spotted stealth masters of the jungle, known for their agility and sharp senses. they're expert climbers and love to rest in trees. Leopards are powerful and can carry prey up into the branches.

COLOR TIP

Leopards have golden fur with distinctive spots. Mix shades of gold and brown for a realistic leopard coat.

RED PANDA

- Class: Mammalia
- Order: Carnivora
- Family: Ailuridae
- Origin: Eastern Himalayas

Red pandas are like the furry acrobats of Asia, with fluffy tails and a taste for bamboo. they're great climbers and spend a lot of time in trees. Red pandas are known for their gentle and playful personalities.

COLOR TIP

Red pandas are reddish-brown with a white face. Highlight their unique appearance with these colors.

SQUIRREL

- Class: Mammalia
- Order: Rodentia
- Family: Sciuridae
- Origin: Worldwide

Squirrels are like nature's acrobats, with fluffy tails and a love for climbing. They dash around trees and zip through the air like tiny superheroes. Squirrels collect nuts and seeds, storing them in secret spots for a later snack.

COLOR TIP

Squirrels are often brown or gray. Use variations of these colors and add a fluffy tail.

TOUCAN

- Class: Birds
- Order: Piciformes
- Family: Ramphastidae
- Origin: Central and South America

Toucans are like the rainbow-billed flyers of the rainforest, with big beaks and vivid feathers. They love to eat fruit and are excellent fliers. Toucans are known for their striking looks and playful nature.

COLOR TIP

Toucans have striking black bodies and vibrant beaks. Make their beaks pop with bright colors.

SALAMANDER

- Class: Amphibia (Amphibians)
- Order: Urodela
- Family: Varies
- Origin: Africa, Madagascar, southern Europe, and Asia

Salamanders are the forest's slippery surprises, with shiny skin and wiggly ways. They love to hide under leaves and logs, near cool, wet places. Some salamanders can even regrow their tails if they lose them, like magic lizards of the woods.

COLOR TIP

Salamanders come in various earthy colors. Use a mix of browns and oranges for a natural look.

TIGER

- Class: Mammalia
- Order: Carnivora
- Family: Felidae
- Origin: Asia

Tigers are the fiery and fierce hunters of the jungle, with orange coats and black stripes. They're expert swimmers and are known for their strength. Tigers are top predators and have a roar that can be heard from miles away.

COLOR TIP

Tigers have orange fur with black stripes. Emphasize their stripes with sharp contrasts.

DOLPHIN

- Class: Mammalia
- Order: Cetacea
- Family: Delphinidae
- Origin: Oceans worldwide

Dolphins are the playful swimmers of the sea, with sleek bodies and a love for leaping. They're intelligent and live in groups called pods. Dolphins use clicks and whistles to communicate and have a smiley appearance.

COLOR TIP

Dolphins are typically gray with a light underside. Create the illusion of their sleek bodies with these colors.

PYTHON SNAKE

- Class: Reptilia
- Order: Serpentes
- Family: Pythonidae
- Origin: Africa, Asia, Australia, and some islands

Python snakes are like the quiet explorers of the wild, with coiled bodies and a taste for adventure. They are strong and have the remarkable ability to swallow large meals whole. Pythons are typically found in warm places and are known for their slow, deliberate movements.

COLOR TIP

Pythons can be various shades of brown or green, and they often exhibit unique patterns. Experiment with different snake patterns and colors to capture their appearance.

COUGAR

- Class: Mammalia
- Order: Carnivora
- Family: Felidae
- Origin: North America and South America

Cougars, or pumas, are the silent and stealthy hunters of the mountains, with golden coats and sharp eyes. they're great climbers and can jump really far. Cougars are like the ninjas of the wild, prowling quietly to catch their prey.

COLOR TIP

Cougars are typically brown or tan. Play with shades of brown to bring out their appearance.

CHAMELEON

- Class: Reptilia
- Order: Squamata
- Family: Chamaeleonidae
- Origin: Africa, Asia, and Australia

Chameleons are like nature's color wizards, with eyes that can look in two directions at once. They change colors to match their moods and surroundings. These slow-moving reptiles live in treehouses and use their long, sticky tongues to catch tasty bugs.

COLOR TIP

Chameleons are masters of camouflage. Try different colors to depict their ability to change.

FOX

- Class: Mammalia
- Order: Carnivora
- Family: Canidae
- Origin: Every continent except Antarctica

Foxes are clever and adaptable creatures known for their reddish-brown fur, pointed snouts, and bushy tails. They are skilled hunters and often live in family groups. Foxes are celebrated in folklore for their intelligence and cunning nature.

COLOR TIP

Use warm shades of red-brown for their main body color. Include white on the chest and paws, dark brown or black on the legs and ears, a white tip on the tail, and bright amber shades for the eyes.

KANGAROO

- Class: Mammalia
- Order: Diprotodontia
- Family: Macropodidae
- Origin: Australia

the kangaroo is an amazing marsupial known for its strong legs and bouncy tail. kangaroos are like nature's jumpers! they eat plants, carry their babies in a pouch, and often live in groups. kangaroos are like the athletes of the wild, always on the move.

COLOR TIP

kangaroos are often gray or brown. use different shades to bring out their fur texture.

OWL

- Class: Birds
- Order: Strigiformes
- Family: Strigidae
- Origin: Every continent except Antarctica

Owls are like the wise creatures of the night, flying silently and hunting with sharp beaks. They can turn their heads almost all the way around. Owls are known for their big eyes and hooting sounds.

COLOR TIP

Owls can be brown, gray, or white. Highlight their feather patterns with these colors.

OTTER

- Class: Mammalia
- Order: Carnivora
- Family: Mustelidae
- Origin: North America, Europe, Asia, and Africa

Otters are like the playful swimmers of the rivers and oceans, with sleek bodies and webbed feet. they're known for their love of water and can do tricks like rolling and diving. Otters are expert hunters and use their strong tails to steer in the water.

COLOR TIP

Otters have brown fur. Add some lighter tones for a realistic otter coat.

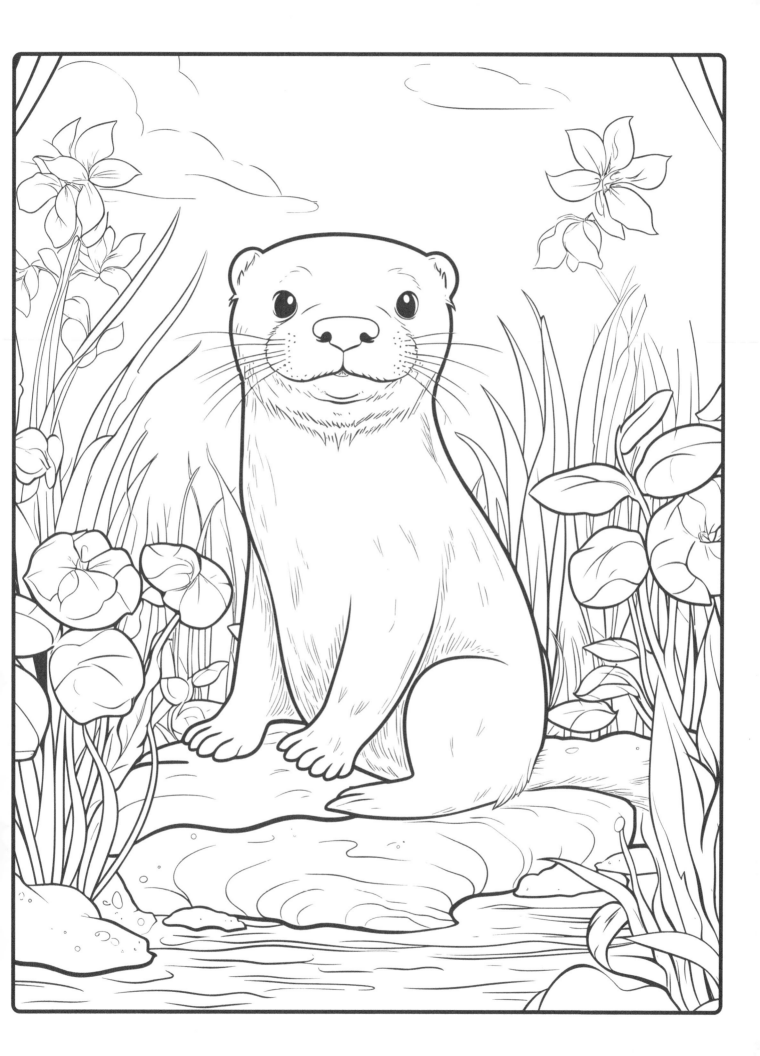

PEACOCK

- Class: Birds
- Order: Galliformes
- Family: Phasianidae
- Origin: Asia

Peacocks are like the kings of the garden, with feathers as bright as the sun. They love to show off their stunning tails, fanning them out in a colorful dance. These fancy birds strut around, making everyone stop and stare at their beauty.

COLOR TIP

Peacocks are vibrant with iridescent feathers. Use bright blues and greens to showcase their striking plumage.

HUMPBACK WHALE

- Class: Mammalia
- Order: Cetacea
- Family: Balaenopteridae
- Origin: oceans worldwide

the humpback whale is a massive and friendly giant of the sea, with a big hump on its back. these whales are incredible swimmers, traveling far and singing songs to their friends. they love leaping and splashing, like acrobats of the ocean.

COLOR TIP

Humpback whales are dark gray with mottled patterns. Create their distinctive markings with gray and white.

CHIMPANZEE

- Class: Mammalia
- Order: Primates
- Family: Hominidae
- Origin: Africa

Chimpanzees are like our cousins in the jungle, with furry bodies and expressive faces. They're super smart and live in big groups called troops. Chimps love to swing from trees, eat tasty fruits, and even use tools to solve puzzles.

COLOR TIP

Chimpanzees are brown and black. Add variations of brown to capture their furry appearance.

HUMMINGBIRD

- Class: Birds
- Order: Apodiformes
- Family: Trochilidae
- Origin: North America and Central America

Ruby-throated hummingbirds are like tiny jewels of the sky, hovering in the air and sipping nectar. They're the only hummingbird species in eastern North America. Hummingbirds are known for their rapid wing beats and iridescent feathers.

COLOR TIP

Hummingbirds come in various vibrant colors. Use bright and iridescent hues to depict their shimmering feathers.

GREEN SEA TURTLE

- Class: Reptilia
- Order: Testudines
- Family: Cheloniidae
- Origin: Oceans worldwide

Green sea turtles are the wise travelers of the deep, with greenish shells and friendly eyes. they're the only herbivorous sea turtle species and love to munch on seagrasses. Green sea turtles are important for keeping seagrass beds healthy.

COLOR TIP

Green sea turtles are a mix of greens and browns. Blend these colors to recreate their unique shell.

FLAMINGO

- Class: Birds
- Order: Phoenicopteriformes
- Family: Phoenicopteridae
- Origin: Africa, the Americas, and Europe

Flamingos are like the elegant dancers of the wetlands, with long legs and pink feathers. They often stand on one leg and love to eat tiny water creatures. Flamingos are known for their grace and unique appearance.

COLOR TIP

Flamingos are pink with long legs. Make them stand out with a soft pink and white combination.

AMERICAN BISON

- Class: Mammalia
- Order: Artiodactyla
- Family: Bovidae
- Origin: North America

American bison, often called buffalo, are like the grand guardians of the prairies, symbolizing strength and endurance. They used to roam the American plains in huge herds and are important for the ecosystem.

COLOR TIP

American bison are often brown. Add depth to their fur with various shades of brown.

COYOTE

- Class: Mammalia
- Order: Carnivora
- Family: Canidae
- Origin: North America and Central America

Coyotes are like the crafty explorers of the wild, with bushy tails and a curious nature. They live in a variety of habitats and are known for their adaptability. Coyotes are important for controlling certain animal populations.

COLOR TIP

Coyotes are grayish-brown. Use these earthy tones to create a realistic coyote appearance.

GREAT WHITE SHARK

- Class: Chondrichthyes
- Order: Lamniformes
- Family: Lamnidae
- Origin: Oceans worldwide

Great White Sharks are the rulers of the ocean's depths, with grayish-white color and sharp teeth. they're powerful swimmers and top predators in the ocean. these sharks are known for their awe-inspiring size and hunting skills.

COLOR TIP

Great white sharks are typically gray with white undersides. use these colors to portray their powerful presence.

Thank you for making it this far!

I deeply appreciate the time you've dedicated to enjoying this book. As a newly publisher founded in 2023, it's a genuine pleasure and honor for me to share this wild journey with you or your children.

Therefore, if you have a minute, I would love to read your impression of this book on Amazon.

I want to know what you take away from it! :)

How to leave your review:

1. Open your camera on your smartphone.
2. Point your mobile phone camera at this QR code.
3. The webpage to write the review will appear in your browser.

Or visit website **tomeudf.com/reviewwild** in your browser.

Made in United States
Cleveland, OH
04 December 2024

11346284R10050